THE GAME OF BALLS:
BALL GAMES ALL OVER THE WORLD

Speedy Publishing LLC
40 E. Main St. #1156
Newark, DE 19711
www.speedypublishing.com

Ball games are any form of game or sport which feature a ball as part of play.

Basketball is a sport played between two teams on a rectangular court with a netted hoop at either end. Basketball is one of the world's most popular and widely viewed sports.

Golf is a club and ball sport in which players use various clubs to hit the balls into a series of holes on a course in as few strokes as possible. The game is played on a course with an arranged progression of either nine or 18 holes.

Polo is an indoor or outdoor ball and goal game played on horseback. The objective is to score goals against an opposing team. Players score by hitting the ball through the opponents' goal using a long-handled mallet.

Pétanque is a form of boules where the goal is to throw or roll a steel ball at a smaller wooden ball while standing inside a circle with both feet on the ground. Petanque is one of Europe's most popular outdoor games.

Bowling refers to a series of sports or leisure activities in which a player rolls or throws a bowling ball towards a target. The target is usually to knock over pins at the end of a lane.

Beach volleyball is a team sport played by two teams of two players on a sand court divided by a net. The objective of the game is to send the ball over the net and to ground it on the opponent's court.

Baseball is a bat-and-ball game played between two teams who take turns batting and fielding. Teams consist of nine players who use a leather-covered hard ball, a wooden or aluminum bat, and padded gloves.

Pool or pool billiards
is played on a pool
table having six
receptacles called
pockets along the
rails, into which balls
are deposited as the
main goal of play.

Football is a sport played between two teams of eleven players with a spherical ball. The objective of the game is to score by getting the ball into the opposing goal.

Cricket is a bat-and-ball game played between two teams of 11 players each. Cricket was first played in southern England in or before the 16th century.

Field Hockey can be played both indoors and outdoors. Each team plays with eleven players including the goalie. Players use sticks made out of wood or fiber glass to hit a round, hard, rubber like ball.

American football is a sport played by two teams of eleven players on a rectangular field with goalposts at each end. The objective of the game is to advance the ball into the opposing team's end zone for a touchdown.

Water polo is a team water sport. A team consists of 6 field players and one goalkeeper in the water at any one time. Water polo is typically played in an all-deep pool.

Netball is a ball sport played by two teams of seven players. Netball is most popular in Commonwealth nations, specifically in schools, and is predominantly played by women.